THINK RICH

THE POWER OF THE MIND BELIEVE IT & CREATE IT

MICHAEL EDWARDS

INTRODUCTION

Do you believe you can think yourself to becoming rich? If you're even the slightest bit skeptical about it, then I am glad you picked up this book. I am about to show you how you can use your mind to create wealth and prosperity. Many of the greatest thinkers in history have had this belief – one in particular named Napoleon Hill. Throughout his life he became one of the richest men in America, with the power of the mind.

Understanding the Law of Attraction and how to have it work in your favor are a few of the stepping-stones to creating wealth. In reality, the 5% of people who are actually rich DO think differently – some of them use a positive mindset and others have the thought of *abundance* constantly on their minds.

You are about to find out the secrets that have been hidden for centuries, and only few people know about.

UNDERSTAND THE POWER OF THE MIND

Just how powerful can the mind be? Despite the tremendous advances of science and technology today, the full capability of the human mind remains suspended on the cliff of uncertainty.

Several studies and researches have been conducted to widen man's understanding of the mind; yet, the more new things people learn about the mind, the more it becomes unknown.

Indeed there is still a lot to know and understand about the human mind; however, from the very small portion of what is known one can already see a tremendously significant power possessed by the human mind.

"Thoughts become things", describes one of the most popular and controversial illustrations of one of the many abilities that the human mind possesses. This idea has received significant attention recently; nevertheless, it is not a product of the contemporary setting. The idea that a person's mind can produce thoughts that would indeed materialize into things has been around for a long time. Historical accounts have even revealed that this notion has been the weapon utilized by most men, whose names remain printed in the book of human successes over the course of history.

WHO THINKS — **The Brain or The Body?**

THE BRAIN IS NOT the thinker. The brain alone cannot produce thoughts. (Holmes, 1926) Free the brain from the human body and it will cease thinking. Even the body is not responsible for the thinking process. A body without a brain cannot produce thoughts. So who is the thinker?

Contrary to popular belief, seeing is not always believing. There are several important mechanisms and processes that cannot be observed by the naked eye and yet their existence is widely recognized. The thinker cannot be seen, but we know it exists because thoughts occur.

With the absence of the thinker/thoughts, the body is oblivious to what is happening around it. The body cannot get sick or hurt. The body will be unresponsive to any stimulus. Therefore, the thoughts are the ones responsible for whatever the body experiences. Consequently, thoughts possess tremendous power.

THOUGHT VIBRATIONS

VIBRATIONS ARE SENT when a person thinks. Thought vibrations are as real as those that manifest magnetism and electricity (Atkinson, 1908). Some people remain adamant about this concept, primarily because thought vibrations cannot be perceived by any of the five senses. Nonetheless, being intangible is not proof of non-existence.

THE POWER **of Attraction**

THOUGHTS ARE A MANIFESTATION OF ENERGY, therefore are seen as a force; the kind that holds the power of attraction. Perhaps the best analogy that can be used to illustrate how this power of attraction works, involves a really influential magnet. Just like the vibrations of thoughts, vibrations created by these powerful magnets are sent out and with enough effort, they can attract themselves to a piece of metal, as an example. Vibrations sent by magnets cannot be seen, yet we know they exist because of the pull they have. In similar manner, thought vibrations, which also cannot be seen, attract whatever the thought may contain provided that there is enough "force" exerted.

According to experts, the brain is both broadcasting and receiving stations for thought vibrations. The mind can be more receptive to vibrations when they are stimulated by positive or negative emotions. When the brain is vibrating at a rapid rate, it is giving the feeling or emotion to one's own thoughts. Mixing these emotions with the thoughts is necessary before the subconscious mind picks up and acts upon the thought itself (Hill, 1937).

HOW CAN THE LAW OF ATTRACTION BRING YOU WHAT YOU DESIRE?

People can speak expertly about the Law of Gravitation, but their knowledge regarding the equally wonderful manifestation known as the Law of Attraction, might not be sufficient enough. This law can play a pivotal role in people's lives considering that it is the one responsible for drawing people to the things they love or hate.

Law of Attraction simply entails that things alike are able to attract each other. Drawing directly into the context of thoughts, Law of Attraction is saying that positive thoughts and feelings will attract positive outcomes and negative thoughts and feelings will attract negative outcomes.

Indeed, the Law of Attraction is directly supporting the idea that thoughts can become things. The possibility of attracting whatever one wants just by thinking about it sounds too simple and unrealistic. Certainly, it is too simplified in this form. If one understands the Law of Attraction this way, chances are it has never worked for him/her, not even once. This is because the process is incomplete. Law of

Attraction requires more than just thinking about a thing or an idea for it to materialize.

COMPLETING **the Process**

AS MENTIONED EARLIER, thought vibrations can be amplified by emotions; thus, to be able to increase the rate of one's thought vibration, it must be mixed with the appropriate emotion. Consequently, thinking about the thing one wants the most must be coupled with the strong positive feeling of attainment.

Although attaching emotions to thoughts seems pretty easy, it is not. Most people fail in this step, primarily because the emotion attached is inappropriate. Instead of the positive emotion, sometimes the fear of not receiving or achieving one's goal might be dominating. In such case, the vibrations sent will attract negative outcomes. This is because the thought vibrations sent in the universe are negatively influenced by the strong feeling of fear.

Visualization is another important factor for the attraction to take place. One must be able to visualize themselves in the state of having received the item or goal already. Putting as many details as possible to the visualization is advisable. If one wants to be promoted, they must be able to visualize how they would feel being the company's new manager.

Focus and consistency are also significant in the process. Sending positive vibrations to the universe must be consistent. The feelings associated with the thought must always be positive so as to attract positive outcomes. Avoiding negative thoughts and feelings is indeed necessary to make the

Law of Attraction work. This part might post some diffi-culty for most people since negative emotions can easily be triggered by different factors, such as stress. Stress seems to be a delicacy found in the everyday menu of life and stress can awaken several other negative emotions in a person.

These reasons make it rather difficult to address this need for consistency in focusing on positive thoughts and emotions. However, there are some ways to eliminate bad thoughts from disrupting one's focus on positive thinking. The key lies in becoming more conscious of the thoughts running in one's mind. Most of the time before one realizes that he/she is adhering to negative thoughts and emotions; his/her mind is already consumed by the negativity. There-fore, to avoid being trapped in a cycle of cynicism, one must immediately orient their attention to something else once negative thoughts start creeping in. One must also be able to identify specific stimulus that triggers bad feelings and thoughts so as to know what circumstances or things to avoid.

Aside from focusing on positive thoughts and feelings, one must also focus only on the things, events or goals he/she would like to have or achieve. If one thinks of the things they do not like to experience, he/she will actually end up attracting that experience. According to the Law of Attraction, the universe cannot distinguish between "I don't want/like" and "I do want/like". What matters and what will be attracted is that which follows these phrases.

This would really sound familiar to people who experi-enced trying to avoid someone or something and ended up encountering that someone or that something. Most of the time, the more people run away from something, the more they seem to be hunted by it. This is because their thoughts are focused on the things they *don't* want - which is further enhanced by *very* strong emotions. Therefore, the universe answers by giving them what is in their thoughts.

This is the reason why one must never think about the things they do not like. Instead one must focus on what they want to have. According to the Law of Attraction, being able to answer the "how" question is not important. One must not keep wondering how he/she will get the thing or goal that they want. Such thinking can only trigger worrying, and worrying is a negative tone which must be avoided.

Being specific is also very crucial in the process. Stating what exactly it is that one wants is indeed necessary to make the attraction work. If one wants money, he/she must state the exact amount they would like to have.

Lastly, and perhaps the most important factor, is believing. This is very crucial to make all the other factors work accordingly. Without the genuine trust and faith in the power of the mind, one can never experience the Law of Attraction working in his/her life. Believing is the most important ingredient and yet is the most difficult to provide for some people.

ATTRACTING **Riches**

AS PREVIOUSLY MENTIONED, the Law of Attraction is not a recent discovery, yet it seems that the formalization of the said notion took place only in the present times. From the moment the concept reappeared in books, several people showed interest, even skeptics. The sudden rise in popularity of the said law among people across nations can be attributed to the very promising and life-changing influence of the law.

The Law of Attraction reveals that people have the power to attract the things or goals in life that they have been dreaming of. There are no limitations mentioned as to what kind of things can be attracted by the power of the mind. It can be anything from a new car, house, or job, a new relationship, happiness and so on. Anything that the heart desires can be achieved according to the Law of Attraction. Don't forget, money is part of the category called anything.

The aforementioned factors are necessary to make the Law of Attraction work together with the proper positive mindset and would definitely help one to translate dreams of becoming rich into reality.

3

13 MASTERFUL STEPS TO BECOME RICH

There are several accounts supporting the idea constituted by the Law of Attraction, among the most prominent include the writings of Napoleon Hill. Hill was born in Wise County, Virginia in October 1883 and passed away on November 8, 1970. He was able to come up with books revealing the key to success. One particular book that influenced millions of people is entitled *Think and Grow Rich*.

In this book, Hill identified 13 steps that would help a person achieve his/her goal of becoming rich (Hill, 1937). The steps/principles include the following:

FIRST PRINCIPLE -DESIRE

According to Hill, the very first step to riches lies in having a burning desire to become wealthy. Such desire must be dominating one's mind for a long period of time. The desire must be definite so as not to confuse it with a hope or a wish. Wishing cannot bring money but desire coupled with a definite plan and persistence can.

Hill offered six specific steps on how one can transmit

his/her desire for money into its financial equivalent. The steps include the following:

1. Being definite with the amount of money desired. Desiring to be rich is too broad. One must be able to fix in his/her mind the exact amount of money they would like to have.
2. Determining what one intends to give in return for the money desired. According to Hill there is no such thing as "something for nothing". To be able to get one thing, you must also be willing to give another in return.
3. Establishing a definite date of possessing the money desired. One must be able to set a particular date in the calendar when they would like their desired money to be received. Once again, being specific is crucial.
4. Making a definite plan for carrying out the desire. After creating a desire, one must start putting the plan into action immediately whether they are ready or not.
5. Writing a statement. The statement must be concise and must include the specific amount of money desired, the time limit for the money's acquisition, the things one intends to give in return for the money and a clear description of the plan that one will use to accumulate the money.
6. Reading the written statement aloud. This step must be done twice a day - once after rising in the morning and once before going to sleep at night. However, reading does not mean just plain reading. One must be able to see, feel and

believe that they already possess the money as they read through the statement.

The sixth step was stressed importantly in Hill's book; and therefore one must be able to follow it accordingly. To be able to easily accomplish the said step, one must have a desire so strong it becomes synonymous with an obsession. A person must be keenly determined to achieve the money to the point that they can already convince their subconscious mind that they are already in possession of the money.

SECOND PRINCIPLE – **Faith**

Believing in the attainment of the burning desire is the next key. According to Hill, faith is a state of mind that can be created and prompted through affirmation and repetition of instructions sent to the subconscious mind. Therefore, faith can be learned. If one finds it difficult to readily trust the notion that his/her desire can really materialize, there is no need to worry. They can just induce faith into their system by declaration and repetition.

Through affirmation and repetition, one is convincing the subconscious mind that he/she believes that whatever amount they asked for will be received. This constitutes the only known methods of developing one's faith voluntarily, according to Hill.

CONSTRUCTIVE AND DESTRUCTIVE *Thought Impulses*

Just like how faith can voluntarily be developed, thought impulses that are repeatedly sent to the subconscious mind will later be accepted and acted upon by the said faculty of the mind. Translating the impulses to their physical counterparts will then follow.

Unfortunately, the subconscious mind cannot discriminate between a constructive and a destructive thought impulse. Therefore, one must be wary on the kind of thoughts dominating in his/her mind for destructive thoughts can materialize.

This is the main reason why poor people tend to get poorer while rich people tend to get richer. Millions of people who are submerged in poverty usually develop a kind of thinking that they are doomed to poverty and failure. There exists a widely held belief that people's poverty is controlled by some strong force that is outside themselves. Such thinking is dangerous because such strong beliefs can be picked up and acted upon by the subconscious mind and translated into their physical equivalent.

Rich people are generally not bothered by such thinking. Worrying about finances is not the dominating thought vibrating through their minds. Usually their thoughts are filled with matters like; what else would they want to have, places they would like to go or additional businesses they would like to try. Rich men and woman usually have thoughts that are not accompanied by negative emotions such as anxiety and fear. Hence, the rich gets richer.

THIRD PRINCIPLE – **Autosuggestion**

Hill characterized autosuggestion or self-suggestion as self-administered stimuli and recommendations that can reach the mind through the five senses. Autosuggestion plays a pivotal role as it communicates with the conscious and the unconscious mind. With autosuggestion, one is deliberately convincing themselves that the desire will materialize. The goal of autosuggestion is to make the thought dominate so as to reach the subconscious mind so it can be translated into its physical equivalent.

To fully understand how autosuggestion works, one can just compare it to telling a lie repeatedly. The more often the lie is uttered, the more it seems to be real and to no surprise, it will later be accepted by the person as a fact. With autosuggestion, what a person feeds their mind eventually becomes real. When allowed to dominate their thoughts, they come alive.

The self-suggested instructions must be accompanied by emotions and faith. This is primarily because words plainly uttered do not reach one's subconscious mind.

THE FOURTH PRINCIPLE – **Specialized Knowledge**

Hill offered a relatively new conception to being an educated man. According to Hill, an educated person is the one who has developed the faculties in their mind which allows them to attain anything that they want without violating other people's rights. Education must be organized and directed wisely through concrete plans of action to the certain end of receiving the money, if it is money that one desires.

Specialized knowledge is necessary to assure that one has something to offer in return for the money desired. It could be in line with merchandise, services or profession. It can be taken from a university or just in everyday experiences. According to Hill, what's important about education is that it can be translated into practical purposes.

· · ·

THE FIFTH PRINCIPLE – **Imagination**

What one cannot see in their mind, can never land in their hands. Imagination plays a pivotal role in utilizing the power of the mind. As characterized by Hill, imagination is the one responsible for giving desires their forms and actions. Without imagination, visualizing that one already owns that which they so desire can never be accomplished. Furthermore, plans for the acquisition of that which is desired are created and organized in the faculty of imagination.

Hill mentioned two forms of imagination in his book, called synthetic and creative imagination. The former refers to the faculty that works with old ideas, concepts and plans to come up with new combinations. The latter is the form of imagination where new ideas are created. This is the faculty through which the finite mind of a person communicates directly with the "Infinite Intelligence." Creative imagination works automatically and functions only once the mind vibrates at an extremely rapid rate.

THE SIXTH PRINCIPLE – **Organized Planning**

The formation of organized, definite and practical plans constitute the sixth step mentioned by Hill. Cooperation is important in organized planning because it will involve the presence of other people. According to Hill, no individual cradles sufficing experience, innate ability, education and knowledge that can ensure the great fortune accumulation. Thus, his suggestion is for one to form an alliance that would create and carry out the plans to achieve the goal of fortune.

Part of this plan-making stage is to devise a strategy that can be utilized once failure is experienced. Being disheartened is common for most people who encounter failure. Nonetheless, one must keep in mind that failure only means that something is wrong with the plan and in a way, meeting failure can be helpful for one to end up with a polished plan that is surely effective.

THE SEVENTH PRINCIPLE – **Decision**

This part suggests that everyone must do away with procrastination, which is the opposite of decision. People who have accumulated fortunes share a commonality among each other. They tend to decide quickly and change their decisions, sometimes slowly. On the other hand, people who have failed to accrue money, make decisions slowly and change them quickly.

Decision-making, according to Hill, must be done solely by the person involved. If one can easily be influenced by other's opinion, they can never have a desire of their own. In cases where facts are needed to be gathered from other people before the decision can be made, one must secure the facts without unveiling to anyone the underlying purpose of doing so.

THE EIGHTH PRINCIPLE – **Persistence**

Will power is the basis of persistence. Without this quality, one is already defeated before the battle even begins. Hill mentioned definite causes upon which persistence is based and these causes include; certainty of purpose, co-operation, self-reliance, accurate knowledge, will power, desire and definiteness of plans and habits.

. . .

DEVELOPING **Persistence**

Not everyone is gifted with perseverance. Some people just lack determination in everything they do. Nonetheless, if one is serious enough about their goal of accumulating riches, developing persistence is a must. Here are some of the necessary steps to develop persistence as provided by Hill in his book *Think and Grow Rich*:

1. Having a definite purpose supported by the burning desire for its fulfillment.
2. Creating a definite plan that is expressed in incessant action.
3. Having a mind that has the strongest barrier against all discouragements and negativities encountered.
4. Forming friendly alliances with other people who can offer encouragements for one to stick with the plan and purpose.

THE NINTH PRINCIPLE – **Power**

Power is responsible for translating the plan into action. Hill defined power as organized and intelligently directed knowledge. According to him, greater power can be gained through the Master Mind. He also offered a definition of the Master Mind, "the coordination of knowledge and effort, in a spirit of harmony between two or more people, for the attainment of a definite purpose". (Hill, 1937)

THE TENTH PRINCIPLE – **Sex Transmutation**

Sex transmutation is defined by Hill as the changing of

the mind from thoughts of physical expression to thoughts of some other nature. Desire for sex is said to be the most powerful of human desires. Such desire can make men develop courage, will power, persistence and eager imagination. All these combined can be utilized to create a very powerful force. Hence, the idea behind sex transmutation is harnessing the strong and impelling desire for sex and redirecting it along other lines such as arts, literature and even accumulation of riches.

THE ELEVENTH PRINCIPLE – **The Subconscious Mind**

The subconscious mind sends and receives positive and negative thoughts. From what has been discussed in this book so far, one should have a clearer picture of the functions of the subconscious mind. Drawing from Hill's conception, a person can voluntarily plant a thought in his/her subconscious mind. One cannot control the subconscious mind but can hand over the desires one would like to translate into their physical counterparts.

THE TWELFTH PRINCIPLE – **The Brain**

The brain serves as the broadcasting and receiving station for thought vibrations. The brain, through its medium, can attract thoughts coming from other brains. This happens when rapid vibration is present. The brain sends the thought vibrations of the person through its sending station- that is the subconscious mind.

. . .

THE THIRTEENTH PRINCIPLE – **The Sixth Sense**

The sixth sense is what Hill has been referring to as the Creative Imagination. It is a part of the subconscious mind through which ideas, thoughts and plans flash. This is the part of the human mind through which Infinite Intelligence can communicate voluntarily without necessary efforts exerted by the person. Nonetheless, this could only happen once the sixth sense, together with the twelve other principles mentioned has been mastered by a person. According to Hill, the sixth sense defies description and only when it has been mastered can one fully understand it.

4

STRATEGIES TO KEEP A POWERFUL MINDSET & MAKE IT HAPPEN

The Law of Attraction and Napoleon Hill's Thirteen Steps to Becoming Rich both suggest that keeping a positive mindset can really help a person become rich. Even simple everyday experiences would teach one that a single negative thought enhanced by some powerful emotion can cause more bad events to come his/her way. While a positive thought seem to attract good news.

The mind indeed carries some mysterious power that based on what is currently known and can take people to the reality of their desires.

A positive mindset can even provide a person health benefits. Research shows that a person who maintains a positive outlook in life experiences the following; greater resistance to catching colds, sense of well-being and improved health, reduced risk of heart diseases and lesser risk of developing stress-related ailments.

BELIEVING **in One's Self**

The essence of a positive mindset lies in the trust and

belief one bestows to his/her own self. Indeed, the concept of self plays a central role in determining how a person views their worth as a person.

The way one perceives his/her self is largely influenced by their childhood experiences. Fortunate are those whose parents were able to teach them how to trust their own selves. Nonetheless, not everyone was told at an early age that they are beautiful and capable. This is one of the main reasons why some people develop a negative notion of their own selves, which directly influences all the aspects of their lives.

If one sees themselves to be unworthy, then they will be. This, to some extent, is a self-fulfilling prophecy. The human mind is powerful enough to materialize whatever is dominating in one's thought. Thus, developing a better view of one's self is crucial.

One must get rid of self-doubt because it can easily devour a person's confidence. Usually there are voices coming from the inside that tell a person that they "cannot". This holds a very strong power over the person, primarily because it is an internal insecurity.

To get rid of self-doubt, one must start confronting it instead of submitting to it. Being mindful as to when the doubts occur is important. This is because such a negative thought must not be allowed to linger in one's consciousness. Hence, at the onset of the thought, one must immediately find a way to dissolve it. A recurring doubt must be dealt with. When a person hears the doubt from within, they must assess it. Where is the doubt coming from? Why is there such a doubt? Knowing the source can be very helpful to finding an appropriate aid for such a negative thought.

Answering the self-administered doubt is the next thing

to do. If the voice inside tells a person he/she cannot, one must answer "why not". After which, one come up with a list of several reasons falsifying the doubt. One must keep his/her focus on that said list. Reading the list repeatedly can make the "I can" thought dominate in the brain and can eventually eliminate self-doubt.

Aside from the voice within, people outside one's self can actually throw doubts at a person. This is another main source of self-defeating disbelief to one's self. Sometimes, people think that a person cannot do a thing, not because they know that the capabilities of that person are insufficient but because they are just convinced that everything is impossible. Indeed, some people are inveterate pessimists and listening to what they say is one of the biggest mistakes one can make.

There are several people who can offer negative perceptions to a person. Sometimes, these people are even considered by the person as his/her significant others. Opinions or doubts coming from outside of the self cannot be controlled by the person; nonetheless, how these would influence him/her can definitely be decided upon by the person alone.

Only the person knows himself or herself best. No one else can identify in pure exactness all the traits, capabilities and even weaknesses that a person possesses but him/her. This is the main reason why doubts from other people must not be allowed to alter one's perception of themselves. The journey one is traversing is unknown to other people; thus, they cannot, dictate that which a person can or cannot accomplish.

The mind is wired at responding to reason. Thus, when faced with doubts, a person just needs to feed the mind with reasons to believe instead of distrust.

5

DEALING WITH FAILURE

Perhaps the most difficult part of trying is failing. For instance, one may try every step mentioned in the Law of Attraction and that of Hill's principles yet end up with nothing but a broken hope of becoming rich. This failure can be the sole reason for the person to give up all their faith with the promising power of their own mind. Some people can really be so disheartened over a single failure that a second trial is way too scary to consider. What people must be reminded of is that the greatest achievements recorded in the history of humankind were completed successfully after several trials and failures. Failing is a necessary evil for a person to grow.

Most people are afraid of failure primarily because it has the power to bring strong feelings of being foolish, useless and incompetent. Nonetheless, failures can always happen to anyone at any time or place. What one must learn is how to handle the situation accordingly.

A positive mindset can eliminate the fear of failure. Everyone experiences failures; yet people differ on how they behave after said experience. This is because people differ in the kind of outlook they utilize to view their life events. In reality, what matters is not what one experiences, it is how one reacts to such experience. Thus, changing one's mindset regarding failure is the key to effectively handle them.

Failures are opportunities for people to improve themselves and aim for the better. Instead of fearing failure, people must consider it as a challenge. This way failure itself will serve as a motivation for people. Indeed, there are several ways on how one can view failure aside from it being the dark and scary experience. Moreover, there are plenty other ways on how one can deal with the said experience.

One of which includes not taking failure personally. Failing is an experience that describes one's interaction with the world. It is never about the person; thus, it must not be taken personally. One must learn to be objective with his/her experiences.

If one does not want to encounter failure, then they must stop thinking about it. Sometimes people fear failure so much that they unwittingly are making it their goal. Focusing too much on failure will result in its manifestation.

Lastly, one must develop his/her perseverance. Quitting after a failure will lead a person nowhere; on the contrary, a person facing failure straight in the face is courting the greatest success.

AFTERWORD

Along the course of the history of humankind lie incredible stories of ordinary people doing extraordinary things. Can such an incredible story be part of your life story too? Can the mind really be that powerful? Can wealth really be attracted by the power of the mind?

After reading the entire book, the answers are within you already. Believe and you will receive it!